For π –

the incalculable ratio of your friendship over time has run
this string of numbers.

Charles Edward Fremuth

STUDIES IN SMOKE

AUSTIN MACAULEY PUBLISHERS™

LONDON • CAMBRIDGE • NEW YORK • SHARJAH

Ordering Information
Quantity sales: Special discounts are available on quantity purchases by corporations, associations, and others. For details, contact the publisher at the address below.

Publisher's Cataloging-in-Publication data
Fremuth, Charles Edward
Studies in Smoke

ISBN 9781638291985 (Paperback)
ISBN 9781638291992 (Hardback)
ISBN 9781638292012 (ePub e-book)
ISBN 9781638292005 (Audiobook)

Library of Congress Control Number: 2022913143

www.austinmacauley.com/us

First Published 2022
Austin Macauley Publishers LLC
40 Wall Street, 33rd Floor, Suite 3302
New York, NY 10005
USA

mail-usa@austinmacauley.com
+1 (646) 5125767

Table of Contents

"Toute Pensée émet un Coup de Dés."

—Stéphane Mallarmé

"All Thought casts one Toss of the Dice."

—J.D. McClatchy (tr.)

Adam's Making

—after Yeats' "Adam's Curse"

The dogs smelled it—some rattling
        scratch. I shot you a look.
"So far my new boss rubber stamps
the risk as if she's played no part.

"The oldest irony in the book—
        whatever form it takes,
love of work or working at love—
we overreach the real for the fake."

You said, "But if it's love it's real.
Although you mince around at work,
        mastering new dance steps,
she hums the company line by heart."

Like you and me, whispered the pause.
        Like gender and culture;
the open range, the safer paths.
Closed gates, unlocked, domesticate.

"Any curse is our own making,"
        I said, "and work enough

to free the other from tether's end."
Twilight leaned into the shadowed hush.

We felt the moonless sunset pressing
        close as a naked scent,
till barking, scrambling dogs flushed out
the raccoon whose head was stuck in a jar.

Tongue And Groove

the Idea was
to fill your father's desk
with poem after poem
of the flesh made Word
whether anyone bought it or not

but i couldn't
fulfill half my promise
cooped up in a smoky room
with too many distractions
and one Small wonder

all i could do
was weigh down the deep drawer
with reams of recycled
re-envisioned nights
that cracked the tongue and groove

the point is (sorry)
not that the deep drawer
doesn't close right
(a bit askew like me)
and sticks when it slides

just let it be
your father's desk drawer
full of the slow struggles
of the troubled son
he never had

After Picasso's *Sleeping Peasants*

They sleep on shafts of grain, detached,
Though his firm hand lays its red touch
On her restfully upraised arm.
He shades himself from the high sun
With the straw hat of the sower.
His hard-edged elbow embedded
In hay carves its niche like a plow.

She opens herself to the sun,
Opens the green vale of her skirt,
Opens the cream clouds of her shirt,
Opens the two-petaled flower
Of her small mouth to the high sun.
Pure and intact, they dream paused dreams
At peace in the creative act.

Living Here

fleeting thought exiled to flight
the swooping bird's illusion
crashed against the glass

so the unread will rewrite
the tricks to sound out loving
crashed against the glass

of the floating world's peep show
where no airborne dive is spared
the joke (i don't get

but laugh at — lowing to know
healing remains in repair)
yesterdays fly yet

the poor thing left a house gift
its wingspan's ghostly imprint
'This is not your home'

The Face Of God

Kismet? (Praise Him) Allah?
The caterer's boy gets a look
    At Iblissa nude in her spa.
Naturally, he's hooked

    And sleepless out of spite
For everything beyond his grasp.
    So he moonlights at open mics
Putting the Qur'an to rap

    Profane, derisible,
Free-styled, by his heart's mad dancing:
    The Tongue of the Invisible
He calls his hip-hop trances.

    One gig he's overwhelmed
By Homeland Feds and arrested
    For coding plots to sleeper cells.
Without counsel, questioned

    Non-stop for forty nights,
Broken down, he hallucinates
    That they're offering Paradise
If he will cooperate.

So he frames Iblissa,
Gives her up as foreign agent
        Of her imam who launders his
Covert aid to insurgents.

        As Feds trace the assets,
They position the rat rapper
        Undercover to capture facets
Of what's about to happen:

        New pool boy now to lurk
By the zemzem she sanctifies.
        Wired under his Hawaiian shirt,
His Speedo rank and defiled,

        Desire flickers. Sunlight
Glimmers off the hoop of the skimmer.
        Winking blind, he finds her lying
Oiled to a lustrous shimmer

        In a string bikini—
Triangles clasped to moist bronzed flesh.
        And she whispers, "Want what you see?"
Is it a taunt or a test?

        He thinks he wants the truth.
But freedom too. No. Her body.
        Her wealth. No. The greatest beauty.
He cries, "I want to see God!"

"Then take up the jihad,"
She says. "You must serve my master.
Then you will see the face of God.
But never dare to ask for

Me again." He concurs
And serves … and forty years flash by
Like a bucket of buttered popcorn
Before he presumes to ask why—?

To what end had he obeyed?
His severe imam keeps prating,
"Patience! You shall be shown one day
What is revealed from waiting."

Fed up, he leaves his master.
Luckless, hungry and sleepless since,
Homeless by the campfire, fasting
At prayer, he conjures the jinn

Or his muse to return.
But it's Iblissa in the fire,
Her dance in the flaming burka:
"Now what is it you desire?"

"Like a drunken ant
I want to hunt the elephant.
With arrows of water I aim
To put out the sun's flame.

"Like once the wife of Lot,
I want to turn my gaze by half
On the forbidden face of God.
I want one good last laugh."

One More

—for Sara

i came back
seven times
nothing worse
waking up
now i'm back

one more
don't-know-why day
one more
get to friday
one more
hour souring ours

one more
dumb-and-short day
one more
of my forté
one more
heartbreak heyday

i came back
seven times
nothing worse

waking up
now i'm back

one more
fill-in after
one more
know-i-have-to
one more
blank between the dots

one more
empty day full
of one more
odious trifle
one more
endless wish

seven times
one plus more
something worse
there's the next
the stop watch

Still Lifes

—for M. H. S.

Here I sit
on part of your inheritance,
the upper flat
I rent out now,
on the slant of the screened porch—
cushy nest
of our freer times, the nineteenth hole
for a nip as high as the treetops,
squirreled away among squirrels,
and crocked as crows—
you and me against the world
making book on tomorrow.

Here we sat
late, goose necked as the lamp,
betting which watchful spider grabbed
the fly we didn't care to swat.
One morning a cicada on the pine bark
metamorphosed,
splitting its flaky husk
for green wings heaving,
pumping and priming for flight
from sagged cobwebs on the screen,

nearly dried
when bees swarmed on it head-first.

Here we sat
on this house's rounded shoulder,
watching jays and cardinals losing
apples to the crows
whose numbers overcame the others
(chased like you).
The backyard now is all black birds.
Years without
so much as *'Hey!'* when yesterday
'Words fail' on university stationery
(with lozenges for coarse hoarse talk)
arrives close on sticky weather.

Here I sit
where easy living loops backwards
to make the heart of memory queasy,
where merely landing right side up
settles the guts to the echoes
of all the seasons
departed as simply as passing reasons
for putting aside whenever and once.

Here is cubed
long-gone summers loved,
these numbered summer days,
and summer on some porch to be.

The Bud

—after Pound's "Plaint"

In my garden greener
        than green desire,
Butter-petaled cries
In riotous blossoms
Rise on rosy breezes
To embrace the next bud's
        freshest leaning
Toward a purer color.

        O whitening bud!
Braver than love,
More fragile than the fragrance
That draws me tenderly to
Those as you awakening
To morning's whispering patter
        Of showers stirring
Flowers to brightening.

        O whitening bud!
Rooted as tendrils of tears
To the violet pith
Of the blood stem lifted
To bloom this whitening June,

Restore the idle shoots
       In my heart's garden
To open closely to you.

       O whitening bud!
Deeper than dreams'
Desires, warmer than rumor,
I have come back to listen
To you, your hush, after storms
Of longing told me no.
       O whitening bud!
Fill me with the stillness

       Wiser than peace
To curl with the cool breeze.
Already ashen, the taste
At my core darkly clamors
Loud and foul and hollow.
Do I gather no more than
       one whitening bud Cut—
and paling to yellow?

Here It Is

My sister knows some places never mentioned.
Last year Ecuador, not from her portfolio,
She hands me folklore, *un cuadro al óleo*:
Flat peasants dabbed in oils on goatskin stretched
And tacked to the back of a marquee-festive frame:

An ageless meeting in a few bright inches.

In large white strokes, and plain, the fauvist's name.

A man and woman, both weary-eyed and burdened,
Meet under condors near her mountain shack.
About to speak, she plants her walking staff;
About to trade, he bulges bags he's shouldered.

'Imagine what on earth they brought,' I ask.

She shrugs, *'They carry their hope on their backs*
And like it that way. That's the task.'

The Homebody

He won't give up his ornery,
        Hidebound, egocentric ways,
          Nor fit
       As snug as once today's
World news into his own four corners.

He won't like what's been bought or sold
        Nor spare good feeling by his language.
          Most of
       His jests, projected anguish;
All of his opinions, facts retold.

He wouldn't think to bite his tongue
        If it's turned a phrase to death.
          What's felt
       Must find the means to express itself—
Most times up a ladder of lost rungs.

Who feels what moves him hears what must
        Be unsaid or undone by saying.
          Who knows
       Him finds him fond of staying
Home with those whom he has learned to trust.

The Estate Sale

One bluesy shutter clapped against the field stone.
Crude signs led strangers to the cellar door
Unhinged. The warped descent let visitors in
To smell the roots unearthing cobblestones.

"I'll tell you what attracts this crowd," she spoke
As sure as secrets. Other browsers scanning
Collectors' tins and raking through the crates
For Americana leaned in to listen.
"It's not so much to find a bargain. No.
No matter who, however high or low,
A life falls into pieces. So, to pick
Up after someone means that you're in touch."

She took his hand. Together up the stairs
They found the dining room a peeled shell
And walked the hall of faded floral walls
Where patches grouped in patterns long-arranged
Left bright wallpaper where the frames had hung.
They joined those shuffling through the crowded
        parlor,
As if to view the reposed. On exhibit,
The family's antique furniture was gathered—
The tables, torchiere, the Deco couch and chair
Were tagged in red and labeled SOLD—redeemed.

The ruddy peddler, loud and clear, exclaimed
The mantle's masonry a dying art
And swore he aimed to haul the thing out whole.

The fat man draped in ragged overalls
Pawed the knotted pocket doors as relics,
But his wife, while cradling toys and glassware,
Elbowed his gut to nudge him along, "You!
Your snoring! No door built is thick enough!"

Enough. He edged away and cornered himself
Before a looking glass of tarnished clouds
Imposing family portraits over his image.
She measured moods by sounding out his sigh
And took his hand to lead him from the room.
Outdoors the open sheds next drew her in,
As well as gawkers, shoppers and free guides.
One fellow posed a snapshot of his son
Seated edgily on the butcher block.
"It's the slaughterhouse. Say cheese! See the Floor?
Them planks let drainage for the muck to run."

His small boy winced, peeking below at mud
Long steeped in the blood of family meals.

"Just one more thing," she said. "Let's see the barn
And stables over there."

                              "It looks locked up."
He stopped. But she went on to have her look.
He took some comfort in their leaving soon

And walked away to wish himself away,
But there a piled quilt as spare as she,
Old bird, bald to the down on the beam
Of the walking plow (its share in dry dirt).
She looked as rough-hewed as the stone façade—
One who belonged. Her clouded-over eyes
        Faced the sunset of her final say.

"Know it was Pa and Gene quarried them stone
To build the add-on big enough for kids.
Too big. When war took Gene and then my Brett
And all the family that was supposed to be.
When peace went sour, Pa didn't talk but swore
For being 'Put to work by womenfolk,'
And sold out bit by bit to meet the debt
On what he'd called our farm of destiny.
No fretting changes what I can't forget—
Bumping into Pa hanging from that tree."

Her reedy voice as thin as thread then trailed
Into the quilt, snapped by interruption.

"Who's she?" she asked.

        "Forget it. Let's go home."
North the towers, the sheets of glass, and west
The shopping mall of red brick walls and south
The brand-new condos' shadows encroached.

At the shutter's clatter he turned to the house
And saw at first a body, though it was
The wagon chain dangling from the giant oak,
The bark grown over the links at the crotch.

Fell So Wild

Used to wonder
why leaves fell wild
Used to chase
the clouds in vain

Used to ponder
why the dog smiled
Used to have a taste
for rain

Used to wander
for sounds to learn
Used to echo
songs from the nest

Used to be fonder
of each step slow
Used to run to earn
the rest

Used to wonder
where thunder rolled
why lightning aimed
to split great trees

Used to conjure
nature to slow
her pace to tame
the wild in me

Hometown Son

I bit on your barb, *"You lie to yourself,"*
And jerked on the line of reasoning, weighing
The fear against the fact. *"How should I know?"*
We never really spoke. You smacked the dog.
Your temper seasoned meals by scorching feelings
And blistered any table talk at home.

I had packed my heart before I left home
And had it shipped like the book of myself
Waking to lectures and jellied by noon, feeling
Liquid as metaphor. I'd lift the weight
Of anger from you and make you my dog
Taught to obey the swift sure hand it knows.

Naturally I learned. I didn't know
How to get free or how to feel at home
With humility, bonded as a dog.
Pariah of your pack, curled on myself,
Back-biting the end bearing my own weight,
I trained on the scent of uncertain feelings.

To hear Mom's flash point—her panic feeling
Sudden fear brought on too late to know
What to do, or how to portend its weight.
It is the call that only comes from home.

Where else could I identify myself?
Gone bad, I came running like a good dog.

       Our family always had a house dog
To trail the worn rugs of resented feelings.
Some said, I looked like you, your double self
Too familiar to ever truly know.
Your chubby son who never quite left home
Found out control amounted to his weight.

I proved useless to the counterweight
Of Alzheimer's. The barking black-eyed dog
At your mind's door hounded you from your home.
Now the house won't sell. Mold and mildew feel
Like bruises on the walls. The buyers know.
Without you, the place is scarcely itself.

       Waiting all alone, no dog feels at home.
Who knows the weight of one self? But I know
It feels homey with my blind dog in the way.

Talk To Your Father

You're back:
        I hear you choke your prayer to Mom,
And I whisper these open-hearted lines
To no one—aloud—lying by myself,
Praying for sleep like a pagan plaything,
Wishing for listeners.
        You're right. Don't take
Yourself too seriously late at night.
Everything changes by morning.
                Waking,
The challenge of a fresh start, the blessing.

Ella, long ill, long pained, dies in her sleep.
So you talk of the proper way to die
As if now it can't surprise.
              But it does.
Called over by Mom, *"Talk to your father!"*
I broker the momentary settlement
And see her bruises when we tuck you in.
I lie in the next room to overhear
Your fears whip guilt and grief to a whimper.

Resigned, you pack nothing for the hospital,
Like Ella dispossessed.
        The baggage of you

You left with us, to sort it out for years.
I still believe you willed yourself to die.
Anchored by restraints, you sat up and rowed,
Hard and steady, because somehow you knew:
Time the finishing line divide what was
From what it is we cannot seem to find.

Mother Dice

My dad killed good feeling.
So I made a toy of thought as child's play,
Something he couldn't break or take away.

My mom nursed, breast-feeding
None (too many so soon), the hollow tones
Of wanting—not her children's, but her own.

My grandma took me in
When I was nearly three to potty-train me,
Her favorite. Later visitations sustained me.

Then none. Stillness. Seeing
Dad cry. No one told me but I knew why.
Her only son's first love I'd taken had died.

Eight kids, movie seats tiered.
"And why can't *you* be like your eldest brother?
Chip in a little for your suffering mother!"

Attention craved, and feared.
Argument. The insisted good night kiss
On the cheek he had slapped, for what? For this?

For trifling forgiveness?
Ah, house-paced Night! Who saves face?
Infantilized,
The broken idols the years have vandalized.

I chose to be childless,
Or the puppet strings got tangled in the dance.
Pet fetish of Mother Dice—to dangle chance.

Taproot

The redbud blooms!
But wan.
How does she know?
Next year,
She too, "our" trees, will be paper.

Light-perched from crown
To crest
Veer birds from bough
To branch
To lodge curt calls of angry rest

Against rude sounds
Next door,
Their receptors
Tasered
By construction, inch hard by inch.

Racket pounds out
Blueprints
Where there had stood trees.
Now birds
Protest more nests of vacant rooms.

Qualia

"The ox and cart make three."
    —Chinese proverb

—for π

It's the three of us mush
        sharing the flushed
engaged familiar spots
overwhelmed at the helm
        of the unremembered
and what is left untouched

Three of us find one dare
        placed on the stair
beside the locust leaves stuck
yellowed and disconnected
        from tree-cast shadows
on morning's lighted landing

Three of us so homey
         long yoked only
to plowing through knowing
the strut of grunts and guts
         it takes to keep going
re-routing friendship's furrows

Now Is Not The Time

Yesterday in Vondelpark,
After we'd mused and jotted fussy through
museums,
I drew as much beauty from beggars, old bunkies
Embraced in sleep on the bench in the sun.

On the train we felt that frail
Brief peace, like theirs, bonded in trust's patient
hunger
For kindness, for kin, for scraps of understanding
Passing as scenery in this beat-up world.

Today in Paris it's hot.
Guest to no-smoking rooms at the noble level
I smoke at the window's guardrail, nude on a rocker,
Pleasantly spent as a used-up model.

Our love, now a thing apart,
Reads like the page before you, fanned as linen
curtains
Billowed on breeze through the bars *sur le rue de
Varenne.*
I pet my habits. You manage desire.

Overnight hard rains rinsed the soot
From these sills and slate walks to silted corners.
Now downriver the old odors clash with present
Perfect tourists taking shots on a stroll.

Pictures beggar experience.
Neither lost nor found, traveling alone, unseen,
The visionary lolls on some balcony or bench,
Imperturbably restored to dream.

Ode To My Left Shoe

Have you seen it, my left shoe?
Why is it rarely the *pair* that's lost?
Not carrion or separated tread
That blots the potholed shoulder ahead

But the lone brogue; or sometimes only
One chukka on top of the heaped trash
        As king of the cast-off world,
Its mute tongue wagging at the tempest
Of drumming pairs conspiring to pass;

        Or the laceless sneaker curled
Beside one weed that climbs the wall—
The footloose and the rooted partnered;

        One galosh in the puddle;
The scarred buck weathering a bender;
The loafer, welt cut and cuff crushed,
Yawning on the bench; the boot busted

At the shank half-buried in rubble;
The red pump a drunken dancer dumped;
One moccasin from some masquerade;
        The single drab sandal beached
To dry alone for the mate that drowned;

44

The flat at the curb, flattened;
The thong's bare print at the wrong locker—
Like a body part severed from shock

That mind endures as loss, the doom
Of the bond now utterly other;
The booty born to boot his mother;
The glass slipper wed to slip her groom;

The saddle shoe unsaddled;
And somewhere my left shoe, as if
Going missing doesn't matter.

The Hinged Word

"You can have intellectual humility
or you can have self-knowledge,
but you can't have both."

— *Dr. Craig Cozad Howard*

Unforgivably
ran scared at the end.
The frankest voice that
ever called me friend,
"Hey, I **love** *you, man,"*

once you lowed to me.
Cheers, the times, context
(all about the text),
I felt unworthy
(Catholic again),

redeemed, but saddened
I could never be
who you were for me—
eyes-on, wise and warm,
sidekick of rare form.

Your teachings reverbed
with the hinged word
I faked with a drink.
Fellow feeling stirred
my shuttered heart to think.

Cheating At Kananaskis

They came to golf
but first they must applaud
the guest speaker's guile:
Imagine, teaching students
to know truth and beauty
by gazing through green gauze
laced to out-of-bounds fences
at the wonders still wild.

Mozart, mawkishly bowed, flirts for a tip.
The 'Bama madam divulges her down-home stew
To the maître-d' mincing simpers to her husband.
In Asian elegance the group on tour
Curtly goes on in turn, rejoining in turn.
Over similar dishes a dance of delicate hands.
Some cover bite-sized smiles from monitors'
Eyes, whose pursed lips frown over teachers'
Chowing down—their frottage of bent elbows
Making waves over Boss's sounding board.

Formal dress falls out. Silks worn loose,
Power ties tight, measure the cultural bridge—
Improvisation the bulwark of contingency
Finessed and gestured as sleight-of-hand.
Cornered, one lone article taps his nib

On the periodical to raise his thought to song;
But he's the cipher rounded, receiving, enclosing,
Standing for Lord-knows-what amid the facts,
     And sits invisibly quiet as a prop—
Like that out-of-bounds fence running the woods.

     Kananaskis
is carved up in golf courses
of taxed beauty marks,
but Mount Kidd mocks us
from Fortress to Fisher's Peak,
from masks of snow drifts
to summits jagged to
shards barren and bleak
by the high wind raking
his shot through hemlocks
to drop in the shadows
by the mellow sedge
drooped over odd rocks—
where angina seizes him.
     He flat collapses.
Skyward, his eyes yawn
in horror, *Really? This is it?*
This cloud my chief mourner?
The wet long grasses fawning
over him unbounded last rites
revive him. He survives
bogey by improving his lie.

'Real Toads In
[Imaginary Gardens]'

"… a place for the genuine."
— *Marianne Moore*

Real toads
(scavengers endangered in low wetlands)
breed only by the dog-starred moonlight
in the reed beds of brackish marshes
near the tides of to be.
Gulping dank miasma,
the male grumbles in rippled rhythm
as the female splashes
the shallows' silt to prep with him
their nursery.

Real toads,
from egg to tad, survive off decay, links
in the sure chain of rotting remains.
Prematurely territorial
and predatory
of anything *once* breathing,
they gorge on the goods of the dead
as nature's cleaner—

a way of life that seals, instead,
        their destiny.

        Real toads
through generations of transmutation
adapt to new chemical toxins;
and, quite unlike their unknown enemy,
        pass on the mystery:
        puzzle piece and picture
at once—the pulsing starry dots of
        the vastness patterned
in the croaking bloated squats of
        spent energy.

For Keats

How close a chill your nodding death incites,
Recalling from a second-touching dream
Entangled tensions in the heart's phrasing

Throughout the restless tenderness of night;
Enraptured monastic ecstasy redeemed
In the virgin vale of soul-making, chasing

But echoes of your muse, and storied fame;
Pegasian passions in moth-wingèd flight
To the candlelight, though singed by the flame

Of high romance and maiden shades of death;
Your awkward bow and, writ on water, your name
So wondrous one spring, still catches my breath

At such imagination so sincere,
"Above the ingrate world and human fears."

Note: the final line from Keats's sonnet "O Chatterton! How very sad thy fate"

Wordsworth's Fondest Metaphor

Our "drinking in Nature," our overdoing
Each buzz to binge, our ego-tripping funked
On a bender profit-driven and power-drunk,
Hungover, crashed in old slop and new ruin—
The next tech, our soulless commonality.

Soul? Is it cratered deeply as the moon?
Is it fractaled as the forest's canopy?
Chaotic as the constant pull of the sea?
Or off-beat neurons, hormones out of tune?

I'd rather swarm with dolphins in some song-
Enchanted uncontaminated ocean,
Belonging to the currents swift and strong
And sure amid the wafted play of youth than
Conform to casually willful wrong.

Waiting Room

In seventeen ninety-nine
As tapers by midnight pool
Guttering and saturnine
      Coleridge espouses,
"The silence of the silent house is
So most and very delightful…"

      In eighteen ninety-seven
A common sentence accepted
In a cell profound and seminal
      Oscar Wilde insists,
"Between the famous and the infamous
There is but one step…"

      Us cats in Schrödinger's box
Fathom the final curtain
Hear radioactive clicks
      Model the Big Botch
Under hostile neighborhood watch
Alert to the uncertain…

Dream Drag

.waking, my
neighboring percussion
in rattling iron
rising,
seeing
exits blocked.
Screaming,
"That *there:* Out!"
Meeting,
me and
Missus Old Homes,
by hired men working on
making her bend and

drag a shipwreck

and bend her making
on working men hired by
home's old missus
and me.
Meeting
out there: *"That!"*
Screaming
"Blocked exits!"
seeing

rising
iron rattling in
percussion, neighboring
my waking

shipwreck—a drag.

Certain Rain

"The gods are just, and of our pleasant vices
Make instruments to plague us."
*—**King Lear** (Edgar, V. iii. 171–2)*

Synergy aged to weather infinity
Fuels only the same ingenuity

To thrive on consumption among the deprived:
Younger thumbs still pluck out fond old eyes.

Our sanction of pragmatic civil norms
Screens the tracking of immovable storms.

Still sport of the gods, our flight to the sparks
From the sheerest face in the latest dark.

The climate cleaved to economic ends
(And quality of survival) depend

On when we choose to disabuse ourselves
Of our immunity from consequence.

What if the well-off must compete for more
In certain rain on vastly shrinking shores?

Getting Sun

What time's it? Worked late on
My commitment to these bits...

On getting each letter
Yep-right-special where it sits.

You coyote, Hafiz,
Predawn, your yip-rippled yawns

Woke me—choked on a phrase!
And you laughed at sunrise on

And on and on and

Lake Léman

— after Basho

One reflection once
glissando of sallow geese
    chevron-shadowed lake

    bed of tickled mud
wrinkles under the winter's
    rice paper ice sheet

    thin as endurance
thick packed as the bone-filled earth
    beckoning return

Senescence

Touch

     Unmastered, long winds
breathe formlessness—the Unseen
     authentic as touch.

Smell

     Cherry blossoms transpire
scents wilting to roadway fumes:
     We too pass this way.

Sound

     No second moorings
cresting the roaring currents—
     Dive in! Or we drown.

Sight

     What is change? You see
crab apple branches snowed round.
     Far flung flakes, we cling.

Taste

     There is nothing here
and so much to throw away.
     Close the Buddha's fridge.

In Plain Sight

At sunset
two red-ember pinpoints beam
from the thicket on the berm.

Possum eyes?
No. Raw knotholes' rims staring
from the crab apple's chopped limbs,

unblinking.
It passed, sad as shadows pass,
just so, sun and self and saw.

Not thinking,
I'd lopped two living "slivers
from their material sap,"

root and earth.
Now, by purple dusk opposed,
louder glows the yellow full

moon rising…
Why compose
a mouthful
of silence?

"Row One Way And Look Another"

we're amphibious
born to work as blue-
              tongued bargees
competing in pints
of curses for hire

two hordes our polished
fares "the Bores and Bored"
              brains pickled
as ship bread bolus
in a broth of spleen

"boxers not fencers"
we rarely put down
              our weapons
fists on the pole for
relative bearings

like Kant lecturing
"to have a friend frank
              and loving
who will help us to
correct our judgment"

an honest living
the double life yes
       it's weather-
proof as souls undressed
in prayer together

Note: Lines 6–7 from Byron's *Don Juan.* Line 11 from the *Meditations* of Marcus Aurelius.

Culture Mulch

"I ate civilization."
—Brave New World, Aldous Huxley

The art of the grind
flesh and fiber ground
down by putting up
putting on and putting off
dull to harsh surges
of the dead questions
and dumb options steeped
in more streaming needs

Ah the culture mulch
of perennials
more grist for the will
of honeyed blunders
cut up and served to
humble fresh wonders

So the more of less
the bigger i feel
something *must* be real
happening between
live persons removed
from scenes on the screen

Keep The Faith

Easy to be vague
happily engaged
virtually
all the rage to be
on the next New Wave
of technology

Easy to be Right
Left without a fight
unfortunately
the Peace we need
lies in infinity
that last 'Good-night'

So…?
Keep the faith

Easy to be glib
in love with the ad-lib
        ah oh well
the fibs we tell
Heaven and Hell
like Adam's rib

Easy to be brave
light years from the grave
        in reality
the saved will be
        forgiven
as they once forgave

        So...?
Keep the faith

Capitalizing

I. 2000

The richer won
the electoral vote,
hands in the pockets
of good plain folks.
Son of the old
Boss had a Bro
at the polls—
Oh, what a hoax.
Supreme Court judges
knew what it meant:
the People don't need
two stinking Presidents.
The office for sale,
the buck stops where
too few care
where it went…

Capitol lies
and partisanship…
Capitalizing…
Well, grin and bear it.

So they set it up
to swear him in.
Go on, let it go,
unfair as it is.
        We all know the story
of America's might—
        nobody's right,
just notorious.
Then tragedy struck
from the sky unglued.
The villains they fingered
        but nobody knew
how to bring 'em to justice
        "DEAD or ALIVE"
or how to survive
        the economic dues.

The poor will go fight,
the spoiled will chafe,
the rich will get richer,
and who should we thank
        for the coinage today
and the slogan tonight?
        "Nobody's safe—!"
Take that to the bank.

II. 2020

Stand pat. Stand Right.
Online, ignorant armies clash by night.

Stand tall. Stand in awe.
The leader's status quo is the rule of law.

Stand your ground. Stand ashore.
Stand to duty, firm in the dirty war.

Stand fast to stand out.
Shout out "FREE SPEECH!" whitewashed free of doubt.

"Stand back. Stand by."
You also serve who only stand and wait to save

That blessed minority's richly privileged state:
Justice to rape, the Common Good to enslave.

Money To Me

Well, you can change your mind, but your mind
        changes too.
        It's a sneaky, quiet kind of liar.
Think you read the news? Yeah, it read you too.
        You're a debtor. Another buyer.

        Enthralling money
        All pinball money
        Our windfall money
        You're like money to me

Go on, drain your drink, though you know drink
        betrays you,
        Yapping smack in that coded chatter.
No harm done. Anyhow, who's to blame when
        You don't even know what's the matter?

        The sprawl of money
        The brawl for money
        All false like money
        You're like money to me

Then he shifted his chair and aimed a killer's stare
        At smoke rings that had poisoned his brain.

Easy come, easy go. Whatever you dare,
It'll pass like the kiss of the rain.

The catchall money
All will-call money
Our downfall money
You're like money to me

Y' know, you got what it takes, but it takes all you
        got
        To get past the scramble and muscle.
Well, we all, we got plans. Our plan got you
        slotted
        Between your next move and the shovel.

Come Heeled

Doc was buckin' the tiger
In Denver 'round 'seventy-five,
Carvin' up that cheatin' Buddy Ryan.
But Doc didn't care about it,
Didn't swear a lot about it,
Bridled to courtin' his dyin'.

Doc was wanted for reward,
New Mexico, 'round 'seventy-nine,
For the killin' of that drunk Mike Gordon.
But Doc didn't care about it,
Didn't swear a lot about it,
Lashed to cavortin' with dyin'.

His deal, Holliday never bluffed.
The stealin' was in riskin' enough.
Do or die, another marked card,
Another one-eyed jack
Headin' for the graveyard.

Doc was standin' trial
In Leadville 'round 'eighty-five,
For shootin' that braggart Billy Allen.
But Doc didn't care about it,

Didn't swear a lot about it,
Lassoed to sportin' 'bout dyin'.

Doc was lyin' bedridden
In Glenwood 'round 'eighty-nine.
"Well, the worms won," that lunger was smilin',
'Cuz Doc didn't care about it,
Didn't swear a lot about it,
Saddled with sortin' out dyin'.

"Come heeled,"
Holliday used to drawl.
"Come heeled,
Or don't come at all."

Contact

Sonnet Noir

Heat lightning BACKLIGHTS
                    The thunderhead swells
APPROACHING

                    PAN
                    Bruised seacoast horizon
WIPED then

                    SUPERED in ghostly a/c mists
CUT
                    ESTABLISH AERIAL
                            Swells' Hotel
DISSOLVE
                    To chandelier ballroom
                                    ZIP PAN
Conventioneers with badges red as reasons

OVERDUBBED murmurs
                    Billions secreted
MATCH CUT
                Scarlet Nails' sigh to Higher-ups
The Gold Key her pincers pass to Brute Hand

CLOSEUP

> Her rosy eyes pleading
>> *O! Please!*

REVERSE

> To Brute Hand
> *Us Baby? No chance*

ARC

> She plays him
>> Her parted lips corrupt

The climax with the fact

>> *Heartbreak? I can't*

FADE

> To headless silhouette propped in bed

Trade Winds

From my breezy veranda
this sunset at Saint Pete's Beach
scumbles gold dust over the sand:
sunbathers retreat.

This crouching twilight,
this sky the hue of happy fools,
the humpbacked gulf at high tide
dress up the crescent moon.

Pumped plump—with a plop!—
some beach toy green dragon
fated by the trade winds flops
onto my balcony. Wagging,

this jaunce cartoons
to challenge retired courage.
Heroically, I launch it
in a mindless, monstrous hurry.

Teachers Are Not Facilitators

only mind-mirrors,
watchful equivocators,
multipurpose motivators,
invading evaluators
of furor and fear,
good teachers leave it moot.

they can't make difficulty
any easier.
they *can* foster unforeseen
pursuits of truth,
personal judgments worthy
of life's harder choices,
and chances taken
to think as one chooses.

midwives to self-birthing,
teachers must nurture
the labor of love, the groans
of new growing,
the embrace with self-knowing,
the self-taught future,

but not even the best makes
it easy to hear it:
          the most earnest
voice is also clearest—
the spirit of learning.

Porlock

A man on business from Porlock
Knocked on the calm of a cottage door,
Tore poor Sam from his revelry
Delved into incense-bearing trees

And a damsel
With a dulcimer…
You know Samuel,
He was mad for her—
Her floating hair!
Her flashing eyes!

The thirst for revenge,
The powerless will,
Still baffled
But buffered still
By fantastic passions

And the maddening brawl—
Here comes another laudanum nightfall.
If he can't sleep
Or if he wake,
But a wee drop is all it takes.

Oh man on business from Porlock,
               At your own cost,
               There are places
Of the imagination
Which are better gone lost.

And the man on business from Porlock?
               No curious fame.
None ever heard from him again.
               So we pass en route, in hock,
Engraved, forgotten names.

               The opiate thrums
On the mystery summoned:

               What is to become
Of the unbeloved?

Note: Several lines adapted from Coleridge's poetry

Scrapbook

1.

The gabled front end, ivied brick,
The arched door bolted as a rule,
The original cast-iron thumb
Press worn from back-again welcomes.
Fool thing, the key I seldom used sticks
In the gummed-up wards of the lock.

I don't knock.
The grating announces someone
Let in with the hinges budging—
Unlike my heart.

No one home.
Which is the mausoleum?

2.

When Gramps rapped
the dining table he had handed down,
the sapphire crown of the platinum ring
he wore on his left hand's pinky finger—
that wished-for heirloom passed to me to lose—

        commanded
Respect. Even Dad, wound up, toned it down.
Gramps cleared his smoker's throat, a raspy hum,
And swept his cradling hand, conducting time.
"Love you mama. And papa. Don' be a bum.
        Dot's da ding."

        Old World paradigm.
        Some have to choose.
        I chose the ring.

3.

Family affections that white lies tender
        Soon put the overfed to bed;
        The living room means leaving room
For the den's obsessional surrender.

        Small-town schemer
        i ain't rich or smart
        Small-talk joker
        with a Small backyard
        Small-time actor
        with a bad bit part
        Small-scale dreamer
        but i won your heart

        Small game dealer
        but i always try
        to be a Small-hours thinker
        for a long night's ride

Small beer drinker
but i got my pride
Small-scale dreamer
but you're still my bride

4.

Once we were as close as bed by bed.
Dressed in rag-tag sports pajamas
We shared our Little League traumas
And dreamed of ninth-inning dramas.
        Was discovery the treasure?

Slipping in your socks I lost my footing
On the fast track to callous distraction.
A just cause it was, to fight for feeding
My middle son's wooden satisfaction
To tilt at windmills for pastimes fading.

Now let's not overplay the final scene
Because the fall from grace is what we know.
The authenticity of flawed routines
Will slow the dénouement to steal the show—
Our lives no longer larger for extremes.

        As close as once, as I have said,
We're different now as text from text.
So sensitive to what comes next,
We carry on by gum and guess,
Merely close as words can measure.

5.

To my steps, attic ghosts
sense the breath and the flesh
of the family exile
in this realm out of reach:

My disturbing rummage
through the crumbled dry-aged
slabs of coming-of-age,
abandoned and damaged.

Soon this settled jumble's
A tear-down of rubble.
Going down. The stairs creak
in language I don't speak.

Next

predawn who cares
about anybody's
anywhere
if you're not next to me

waking hour
the plainest
weather's paw
or hammer

bird calls clamor
really they do not sing
we yammer
knowing next to nothing

facing felt
the closeness
of sleep-fed
intimates

let's mate this day
to the tuneable air
to the nesting way
of offering shares

under clouds
skidding reds
that tint our
home-lived shades

On Assumptions of
The Afterlife

The eldest brother posed the eternal scam,
"Aren't we responsible if Chas is damned?

"One thing we know: Non-belief *never* saves.
And Chas traffics in works, *not* the true faith."

A goner by the book and by the rules.
Reincarnation ranks, and Heaven excludes.

After the eldest spoke those points of law,
He deferred to T, who has turned to God.

Slow to grant absolution, feeling trapped as
The high priest defending his profaned chapel,

His eyes closed, hands folded, his breath heaved
large,
He expressed his love and condemned me as
charged,

And then himself, as if it were his turn.
Ah! the real sorrow writhed from myths so stern.
Me, I'm not worth the eternal upkeep.
So be it void or judgment, may I sleep?

Hair Sample

"You trim your beard like a poem
That no one sees—but you again."
What does my bro know anyway,
Whether shaven or stubbly, hmmm,
Scrubbing his next expression?

How closely introspection
Corresponds to identity,
To *"being-in-situation."*[1]
Self-image the imago?
No. "Touch has a memory."[2]

The sting of follicles plucked,
The eviction of the in-grown,
The intorted chin curtain strands
Hiding in folds over the jaw bone
I shall let stand no longer

"Al rough and longe yherd."[3]
Worse, tending to wild[4] near the lips,

---

[1] Sartre, *Being and Nothingness*
[2] Keats, "What can I do to drive away…
[3] Chaucer, "The Miller's Tale" (l. 630)
[4] Milton, *Paradise Lost* (IX, 212)

Petty curls cornered in creases
And sprouting to belong, but wrong
For this tickling specimen.

Something Living

"Truth becomes something living; it lives solely in the rhythm
by which statement and counter-statement displace each
other to think each other."
—Walter Benjamin, The Arcades Project

The shelter of the sofa bed
       Dissolves his encapsuled mind;
The pillows muffle what she said,
       The barring blanket blinds.

Somehow the jitters huddled, caught,
       Salve the sting of dares foregone.
But the shadows are dimly fraught,
       For no lull stops the dawn:

That timely sun through parted drapes—
       Cranky as sudden hindsight—
And light that shafts the eyes to gape,
       "We're *both* wrong, and *each* right!"

Moving onward… Never past it…
       Sand painting insouciance
Cast over the shuffling next dance
       Dealt out like forty lashes—

Less one. Which one, not the question.
    The silent treatment undone,
Run aground, redounded, shunned,
    They reshape their expressions.

Another Broken Sonnet

—for Helge

Go, little birthday song,
Recall me to her in measures
Enraptured by her thousand treasures.

Lull her to sleep when I am gone
Again, duty-bound, nowhere near her.

Softly resound this solo sung
Gently sad as the mourning dove's,
To recount not the years (none dearer)
But rather to reprise this melody's
Feathered whisper, *"Why is it love?"*

Because…
It is she;
Because…
It is me.

Lines 11–14: *"Parce que c'estoit luy; parce que c'estoit moy."* Michel de Montaigne, 1588

Psyche's Eros

—for Jules

When she was purely a child
She did not ever question,
    "What is Love?"
Her tears were tears
    That came and went.
Her sighs were sighs.
    Her smiles were smiles
That came and went.
    All laughter and wonder
Simply that which came to pass.
The embrace was just a hug,
And so she did not question Love.

When she was youthful, wanting
To be older, then she questioned,
    "What is Love?"
Her tears were no longer tears
    That came and went.
Her sighs were not dry sighs.
    Her smiles came hard
Upon laughter forced and chased away.
    Wonder grew to worry
Whence it came and where it went.

The embrace much more than just a hug
She came to question distant Love.

But now she is old enough
To grow younger. Why wonder,
      "What is Love?"
Her tears are simply tears
      That well and flow and dry.
Her sighs and smiles, true and brief
      As sighs and smiles,
Food and drink of touch-and-go
      Sweet or sour, great or small,
At once her own and all in all.
The embrace is now once more a hug
That holds the heart that beats like Love.

Innumerate Love

—for Lynnsy,
on our Fiftieth

No flipped-off fourteen lines can scan the ways
Your curves receive my hands and fill my head,
Nor breathe the whispered arc of your look's sway
Over mine, which strayed with other women
To find nobody feels at-home as you,
Who weighs what you weighed when we wedded.

      Now it's fallen gently into softer
Places. Now I'm much more independent
Than honest, and you are more of both than
I am either, by striking lavish set
Designs to stage our barefaced dialogue.
You've cast me past my scripted early death,
Never wanted children, and raised good dogs
To bond with, if our bond becomes a bother.

My greatest risk, best payoff ever—betting
On you to love me for whoever I
Become. We're coffee and rum in separate beds,
Our conversation close when I'm beside
Myself; when we're apart, our spirit webbed
As threads vibrating moods to take in stride.

Our future fills to flip, like an hourglass
Flashing sparkles over the shifting slopes
Of sandy shapes mounting to our numberless
Tumbling triumphs—the mystery of us:
Your level-headed heart, your straight-out hopes
That brought us here, where I am lost to find
I capture *you*—the way the poets boast,
They catch the breath of love between the lines.

Prayer To My Dog

Now train my mind
To fetch with heart and eye.
By way-to-me or go-by,
      Drive my herd of drives.

Lead me to feel
The look of sound commands—
To sit upright, or stand
      Till brought to heel

Again. Show me
Again how to learn to lie
Down, and to wait at ease
      On absurdity;

And show me how
To show, alert to stay,
Aloof to where we place,
      Alive to now—

The knowing nod
That masters the task together,
Devoted to track forever
      The scent of God

By trailing you.
Now train my spirit to pen
The pain and show the joy—
That'll do.

Lyx's Tracks

Dog soldier through our youth, was it
       Time to put you down so easy?
What sucked you up like a breath?
       And your warmth? What is left?

Time to wrap up our best friend.
       Me, I can't help looking down
At Lyx's wide blank eye—Egyptian style,
       Forever stony grave and unalive.

Time to lay the corpse in the trunk.
       Time to drive it to the vet's freezer.
Time to pretend the ashes end up
       On a bed of roses.

       Other masters' dogs still bark
At my midnight stalking of starker anger,
Gravel crunched to dust, pebbles to powder,
Rattle the chill of the lamp-lit corner.

Spittle winded by this passing stranger.
       There's more. I suck it up.
Her eye… and mine askance as hers in death.
And now no pal at home by the next corner.

No best in show. No truest hardy mush.

No bedside Argos.

What else is left but litters to create?

The bond that breeds and breaks.

Cosmic Architectonics

And still the white sun burns unspent
To bleach from disbelieving eyes
    The human depths that lie

Unburied and rise like myths again;
For the sun brings the burden brought
    With weather patterns long taught.

The sallow moon in perfect taste
Turns her battered rocky face
    To the rushed fret of our race,

Reflecting the dust of far-flung waste
That moves like dream through no space twice
    Between the fire and ice.

Mana Pentimento

Priestess? Angel? Or ghost?
Is love but passing love?
Brute blood believes above
Man's doubt in loving ghosts—
Foremost the ghost of love.

At dance, fine timing leads
By chance to joy or dread,
Our dreams deferred to bed.
The dawn unfolds, uncreased;
Prisoners of hope released.

Those who know best know better.
Waking is a blind date
With that flirt, *love of fate*:
Like Bartleby's dead letter:
Loss, regret *"—can't forget her."*

But if there's grace to bless us,
If weather ain't the climate,
If no one scores or times it,
Then let us each confess it,
Mana plays tag and—*"You're it."*

Michigan March

Will winter ever end?
>   She grew distraught
As the blackout conjured all her darkest thoughts.
Her hands in cold suds, Wednesday's Ash on her
>   brow,

Like her mother once, her frail shoulders bowed
To nature's power, to drudgery, to grouse,
Will winter ever end?
>   Now overwrought

With doubt, her sacrifice and duty fraught
And mocked by chores undone,
>   Bristling, she scowled,
Her fingers numb as Wednesday's Ash on her
>   brow.

Perpetual Lenten chores in a crowded house
And now the clock won't even push the hour.
Will winter ever end?
>   *It's a trap. I'm caught.*

Iced over in the gloom she always fought
Against, the reflection of her gray frown
On soap suds, the ashes smudged on her brow,

She saw her loss of faith, but also fraud
In all that's dust, all earthly promise flawed.
God save my wintry soul!
                    She rinsed her brow
Of Wednesday's Ash and crossed herself for now.

Craquelure

—after Vermeer's *Milkmaid* and *Lacemaker*

Paint and varnish shrink
like the loaf's stale crust.
From creamy windowpanes
one shaft through a hole in the glass
lights her brow and downcast
focus on the coddled pour
of milk modeled in ripples
rendered faintly whiter
by the background pentimento
that obscures her next chore
and the map of a distant war.

The canals' chill connects us.
Sun tricks through cloudy tiers,
and every surface crackles
the way varnished paint ages.

Pinched fingers hold fast
to bobbins and pins
in the embroidered lace
between her unraveled ringlet
and the tangle of bright
threads from the pincushion.

One stitch—the odd loose end—
is taken up, pulled tight,
laid in place as her lidded gaze
upon the ladder of souls
into her seamless night.

What's Wrong

sometimes i abhor what i adore
sometimes i cling like the rose's dew
sometimes i wonder what's wrong
o let's let go and go on free
elsewhere someone will please you or me

we're into ourselves beside ourselves
we're solipsists who craft ourselves
sometimes i wonder what's wrong
we each to each come on some way
squirming like a worm on to a leg

sometimes i'm awfully ugly funny
sometimes my finest kindness clumsy
sometimes i know what's wrong
the art of honesty's fixed game
a con like *Singing in the Rain*

there is so much to one square smile
so much to miss in one square mile
sometimes i know what's wrong
humility hurts and who else cares
too vain to pry too proud to share

Rainout

Insidious under-life, the sooty dim
Plows up the surefire path by push and shove
To stretch beyond the rotted, curling rims
Of mud and twigs to air and sun above.

The picnic haunch to haunch, with sexual guess
Near vying knit brows and worsted eyes,
Shares flattery in friendly feasting dressed
In wine's dear elegance, rare cheese, and rye.

The under-life prepares to burst its spores
More boldly subtle than her look implores,
More pulsing steady at its pulpy stem
Than the hidden, impatient worst of him
That blew his wad and bunged it up. A shame,
He curses clouds and mushroom-loving rain.

Fragment From
Humbert's Autolog

Pick up, you heap of—!
Godspeed my nymphet Budding Beauty
      to safekeeping.
V-Eight, outrun that sex-crazed brooding
      Tailgater. Drive steel to duty!

Steer wanton youth (as
Overheated as you at Ho Jo's)
      past each ruthless
Merging along the neon sideshows
      That gloss her callow eyes aglow.

Beastly the burden,
Growing up in commercial culture:
      each purest urge
Gives sway to the most adulterous
      Gear of conditioned compulsion.

Too soon Nature runs
Her course, her plot of surest ruin.
      Her moment come,
Breeze embowered in a rented room,
      Where all at once, but once, she blooms.

One Veteran Of Vietnam

Yeah, that skinny pale guy,
scaly pink with those khaki eyes
Comes in every lunch rush
but got to have his same spot,
Like some old curled-up dog,
scratching god-knows-what off himself.

Always orders bacon burnt,
one egg over easy and
A double gin,
but Jéfé says I gotta ask so I ask,
'Potatoes? Maybe pancakes today?
Toast, whole wheat or white?'

— So which one? Pick one.
Don' matter. Get 'em. Get in. Get out.
Can't choose,
so he winces showing pink teeth it hurts to see.
Most times I gotta interrupt,
'Okay, the usual?'

Fingers poke at blisters,
pick at scabs on the other hand,
Mumbling something foreign
that sounds sorta rat-ta-tat-tat,

Kinda clenching pink teeth,
urgency in his khaki eyes.

Mumbles sloppy when he's eating too,
so sometimes you see
Gross stuff stuck where there's a missing tooth,
slobber on his lips,
But I gotta stop by his table.
My job to be nice.

'Anything else?'
The worst part is when he looks back at me,
Staring me up and down—not like some guys –
just plain spooky
Like he sees through me.
That urgency in his khaki eyes.

'Okay, thanks.' I leave the check
(and never expect a tip).
Then he takes this gingham
beanbag turtle from his pocket
And careful puts it down
behind some dirty plate or glass.

— So which one? Pick one.
Don'matter. Get 'em. Get in. Get out.

He winds his napkin up
around his blisters and his scabs.
Always the same:
one sharp short whistle like some jungle bird
As he quick points his finger
and shoots his own pet turtle,

Letting go this shivering sigh,
like he's sorry for it,
For what he has to do,
urgency in his khaki eyes.

Contour

iridescent
the beer bubble
at the bottleneck
quivering wobbly
on the rim

brimming shimmers
on sunset's waft
thin shivers over
a globe of rainbows
burst suspense

Quick Cut

Over the steeple's shadow
I ran home.

Who else to tell?
"They shot Kennedy!"

Mom stopped sopping up the mess
At the sink. She looked unwell.

Dad stopped tenderizing beef
In tremors of disbelief.

*"That's **not**
something to joke about!"*

At ten I had no doubt.
*"I'm **not!**"*

Watching Cronkite tear, Dad did too;
Like kids, believed what he's told to.

Yes, You

Bewildered fawns among two dozen deer
Stride slowly, sorted in their staggered row,
Across the grounds. The bucks peer deep as
       snipers,
Yearling muzzles poky by mother's stifle.
One doe, frozen, stares me down, minding two.

                    Thought of you.

She poses us before her bedroom mirror
Which faced the mirror mounted in the hall.
Tunnel vision *Me-Her-me-or-her* shrinking
US-Us-us… out of sight as death… sinks in:
Facing mirrors mirrors facing one wall.

                    Thought of you.

Does Plato's mirrored drunk confess who's what?
Is the celibate addicted to her rut?
The pose the prize—we're all exceptional.
No one obsessive, merely obsessional—
Know-it-alls, sciolists, and sceptics, too.

                    Perhaps you?

Deep reader my muse. On the prowl the minx
Lurks close to dupe me. Perfect murderess,
Alluring, her oracular high jinks,
At playing hard-to-get. But after words
She'll toss me off. Her toy, I misheard her.

> Thought of you.

There is a modern madness, *akithisia*,
Cannot sit still without anaesthesia.
But the cure will kill (*iatrapistia*,
That's how it reads in medical history):
Muddled meds scrum; the unbidden visit comes.

> Thought of you.

As in portraiture's deaf-mute conversation,
The necessary presence in the room
Shoos the swooping whoosh of the raven's wings
To plant surprise—that quiet, brief elation—
A random cast as fickle as the moon's.

Charles Edward Fremuth received a B.A. from Princeton University, where he published in *The Nassau Lit*, and an M.A. from the University of Michigan. He dedicated his teaching career to Detroit Country Day School, where he served as chair of the English department for twenty-five years. The International Baccalaureate Organization appointed him assistant assessor in the Theory of Knowledge and site evaluator of prospective schools (1997–2003). He led workshops in the Theory of Knowledge for teachers and heads of schools in the United States and Canada, and was selected to present "Epistemology in King Lear" at the International Baccalaureate North American Regional Conference (San Francisco 2008). His teaching was recognized in several local articles and by various national awards (1993, 2006–2008). In 2017 he retired to collect his writings.